Remembering
Palm Beach

Seth H. Bramson

TRADE PAPER
PRESS

With Florida's then-ubiquitous coconut palms waving in the breeze, photographer Charles Barron captured this image of downtown West Palm Beach across Lake Worth early in 1960.

Remembering
Palm Beach

Turner Publishing Company
200 4th Avenue North • Suite 950
Nashville, Tennessee 37219
(615) 255-2665

Remembering Palm Beach

www.turnerpublishing.com

Library of Congress Control Number: 2010924314

ISBN: 978-1-59652-657-0

Printed in the United States of America

10 11 12 13 14 15 16—0 9 8 7 6 5 4 3 2 1

CONTENTS

In 1898, the Chicago-based Little Chronicle Publishing Company produced a fine stereoscopic card showing one of the numerous pedicabs known as "Afromobiles" that would, by the 1910s and 1920s, become ubiquitous in Palm Beach. A black driver pedaled passengers around town as they relaxed in their moving lounge chair.

ACKNOWLEDGMENTS

This volume, *Remembering Palm Beach,* is the result of the cooperation and efforts of many individuals and organizations. It is with great thanks that we acknowledge the valuable contribution of the following for their generous support:

Collection of Seth H. Bramson
Library of Congress
State Archives of Florida

PREFACE

When one thinks of, speaks about, or writes the history of Palm Beach, an appropriate reference is that wonderful line from the 1960s, "What a trip." For the history of Palm Beach and vicinities countywide is, at the very least, a true "trip," in the ethereal—and certainly in the historical—sense.

Palm Beach became its own county in 1909 but prior to that was part of what was then a much-larger Dade County. In fact, from 1889 until 1899—when the population of southern Dade County became large enough to return the county seat to the shores of Biscayne Bay—Juno, at the far north end of what was then Dade County (now Palm Beach County) was the county seat.

Nowhere else in America was there a "Celestial Railroad." The 7.5-mile Jupiter and Lake Worth Railroad running through Jupiter, Juno, Venus, and Mars opened in 1889. Oil magnate and railroad developer Henry Morrison Flagler put it out of business when he brought his own rail line into West Palm Beach five years later. He erected a home now considered one of the ten most magnificent private homes in America and built two of the most glorious winter resorts in the nation.

Palm Beach today is certainly more than "just" West Palm Beach or Palm Beach, although the former remains the county seat. It boasts innumerable first-class clubs and residential developments, beautifully maintained private homes, world-class tourist destinations, and numerous museums, art galleries, auditoriums, and concert venues. Home to the fastest-growing Jewish community in America, its population is nearing one-and-a-half million people.

From Boca Raton and the Boca Raton Club on the south to Jupiter, Loxahatchee, and the PGA club and course in the north, Palm Beach County, with its fabled history, is a highly desirable destination for any Floridaphile, writer, or historian. The images on these pages capture the fascinating story of Palm Beach and its vicinity in a unique presentation.

With the exception of touching up imperfections that have accrued with the passage of time and cropping where necessary, no changes have been made to the photographs in this book. The focus and clarity of many images is limited to the technology of the day and the skill of the photographer who captured them. Many will spark warm, personal memories for readers, while others provide a glimpse into an era long gone—when Florida East Coast Railway trains crossed Lake Worth to serve the super-rich "resorting" at the Breakers and the Royal Poinciana and a mule car operated between the two hotels, until the great 1925 fire destroyed the second Breakers. Palm Beach is one of the most recognizable names and locations in the world. These are images of the people, places, buildings, and events that made it so.

—*Seth H. Bramson*

Shown on March 19, 1930, the venerable Royal Poinciana is nearly empty, made obsolete by newer, more modern, "fireproof" hotels, complete with amenities not even dreamed of when the RP was built. Sadly, the hotel would last only one more season, when it was ignominiously dismantled. Its furnishing and fixtures were sold for pennies on the dollar to any and all who had the money to buy them. Although the Breakers, the P. B. Biltmore, the Whitehall, and other properties would soldier on, the loss of the Poinciana was, in many ways, a bellwether of the changes being thrust upon Palm Beach.

THE ERA OF MR. FLAGLER

(1889–1909)

Although diminished because of shrinking schools and changing tourist interests, fishing remains a major draw on the southeast Florida coast. One of the earliest known photographs of the sport in the Palm Beach area—taken March 18, 1893—shows a group posing with their catch of the day, a huge hammerhead shark. They most likely were tourists.

On March 14, 1896, in one of the most famous Palm Beach photos ever taken, a group of very wealthy American tourists posed in front of an FEC passenger train and the Royal Poinciana hotel. From left to right are Colonel Philip M. Lydig, Helen Morton, Gladys Vanderbilt, Amy Townsend, Captain A. T. Rose, Mrs. Cornelius Vanderbilt, Edith Bishop, Mabel Gerry, Thomas Cushing, Edward Livingston, Dudley Winthrop, Craig Wadsworth, Gertrude Vanderbilt, Lispenard Stewart, Harry P. Whitney, Sybil Sherman, and Cornelius Vanderbilt.

The legendary Henry M. Flagler would spend $2 million in 1901 dollars to build Whitehall, shown here shortly after completion. Today, it is considered one of America's ten most magnificent private homes and houses the Henry M. Flagler Museum.

This image, from a late 1890s Little Chronicle stereocard, captures the loveliness of the island of Palm Beach, with its Australian Pine Walkway between the two Flagler hotels, connecting the east (Atlantic Ocean) side and west (Lake Worth) side of the island.

The idea of spending the day fishing in the Gulf Stream enticed innumerable thrill-seekers who kept the charter boat captains busy throughout the winter season. This picture taken around 1900 shows why the charter fishing boat business would increase for years to come.

Now located in West Palm Beach, the Gun Club was originally on the Palm Beach side and was yet another of the numerous venues for sports enthusiasts. Shown here around 1900, the interest in the sport is evident from the number of spectators on the second floor balcony as well as on the first floor behind the participants. During this era, almost all entertainment originated at or was connected to the Flagler System hotels.

The *Palm Beach Post* is a respected South Florida newspaper. Originally named the *Daily Lake Worth News,* it became the *Palm Beach Post* in 1916. One of the rarest Florida newspaper photographs that exists, this image from around 1900 of the paper's printing room brings the era of early Florida newspaper publishing to life.

The Royal Poinciana Hotel was the site of lavish entertainments as well as tennis tournaments for men and women—played separately in those days, of course. Here, around 1900, a group of female tennis aficionados enjoy the game while more than a few onlookers enjoy the action.

The Breakers Hotel and the mule car in 1901. Since the track is on the south side of the hotel, the view is northwest and this is the first Breakers, which would be destroyed by fire June 9, 1903, and subsequently rebuilt.

"Resorting" from Palm Beach's earliest days had its requisite daily moments, one of those being the post-luncheon choices of bathing, shooting at the Gun Club, golfing on the island's links, tennis, an excursion to the mainland, or, for many, the relaxing pleasure of the social time afforded with friends as guests gathered on the Royal Poinciana porch to greet and gossip while deciding what they would have for dinner.

Then, as now, golf was a delight, at least for those who played the game and not "at the game!" In 1905, both men and women are preparing for tee off, with kibitzers off to the right under the palm tree.

Though bathing pictures of early Palm Beach abound, this one is rare as well as important, for it shows the safety line which could be used by those who were not proficient swimmers. The pier, in the background of this 1904 photo, was no longer used by Flagler System steamboats but had a small windmill in place to show which direction the sea breezes were coming from.

This 1905 image shows a busy day at the beach. One sign tries to draw visitors to Alligator Joe's daily performance. The other, in the center of the picture, bears the words "The bathing hours on this beach are 11 to 1 during which expert life guards and boatmen are provided for the safety of casino guests. Please be guided by their advice when entering the water." The casino referred to is not a gambling casino, but, rather, The Breakers' bathing casino.

The rumblings of discontent with being a part of Dade County were getting louder and the former Dade County Bank, shown here in this Resler Photo Studio view, changed its name to the Pioneer Bank before the 1909 secession from Dade County occurred. It is unclear whether the bank survived with its new name through the great boom and into the bust of the late 1920s.

On July 4, 1908, the local Home Guard marched north on Narcissus Avenue. Wilbur Hendrickson, on horseback, is leading the fire laddies and officers of the then-volunteer fire department. A note says the little girl visible at right would later become Mrs. Dunkle but does not give her first name.

Breakers and Royal Poinciana guests were fiercely loyal to their chosen hotel, most remaining as guests at one or the other for many seasons. The Breakers porch, shown here around 1905, was to Breakers guests what the RP's verandah was to its aficionados. It became a wonderful gathering spot each day after lunch and sometimes in the evening when events were not planned.

The initial manned and powered flight of the Wright Brothers at Kitty Hawk was but eight years in the past when John A. D. McCurdy brought his Curtiss biplane to West Palm Beach in 1911. McCurdy's flights with the first aeroplane (the initial spelling) to visit Palm Beach County were for the purpose of selling land, most likely in cooperation with the early Palm Beach–area land developers Harold Bryant and William Greenwood, who were based in Chicago and were publicizing and selling land under the moniker of the Palm Beach Farms Land Company.

TWO NEW COUNTIES!

(1910–1919)

In the early years of the twentieth century, northern Palm Beach County schoolchildren were brought to their places of learning by horse-drawn school buses. Here, in 1911, a group of children of various ages poses with their equine-powered conveyance.

Today, Datura and Dixie in West Palm Beach is a busy intersection pulsing with traffic 24 hours a day. This photograph, taken prior to 1914, shows a peaceful image of the location, with the original Episcopal Church, made entirely of wood.

It is believed that the first public auction of land in Palm Beach County was held in 1912, only three years after separation from Dade County in 1909. Standing in front of the real estate office and "The" Bookstore, which was also a Rexall Drug agency, a group of prospective buyers eagerly awaits the start of the auction.

By late 1912, the Florida Coast Line Canal and Transportation Company, partially owned by Henry Flagler, had completed a good portion of what was to become the Atlantic Intracoastal Waterway, with the section from Fort Pierce south to West Palm Beach newly opened. Tours along the coast were usually heavily booked and the fortunate group on board is enjoying a long-gone view of Florida's once scenic and pristine coastline.

One of the symbols of growth for American cities in the early years of the century was a fully funded marching band, which would participate in parades, holiday events, and other worthy happenings. West Palm Beach was no exception, and their 20-piece ensemble posed proudly for a photographer.

In 1916, Clematis Street, as one of West Palm's most important business arteries, was also used for celebratory parades and other events. Thanks to Byron's Photo, this view of the first Seminole Sun Dance was made and preserved.

Growth brought expansion, and in 1916 the Resler Photo Studio captured this group of enthusiastic and hopeful buyers as they awaited the beginning of a group drawing for lots in Lake Worth (the town south of West Palm Beach, not submerged land in the lake by the same name) and in the Everglades, which, in those days, began barely a mile from downtown, just as it did outside Miami.

This 1918 William N. Miller photograph illustrates changes in bathing attire, as shown by the bare legs of the swimmer at right and diver at left.

Historians owe unending thanks to the early photographers in Miami, Hollywood, Fort Lauderdale, and Fort Pierce, and their contemporaries at the Resler Photo Studio in West Palm Beach, for their stunning imagery and high-grade photo art. Preserving much of Palm Beach County's history on film, Resler even photographed his own studio, shown here on Myrtle Street in a 1917 scene.

"The Coquina"—the name of a famous hotel in Ormond, Florida—was also the name of a houseboat from Massey, Maryland. Photographed by William N. Miller, the houseboat is docked at Palm Beach in 1918.

Although regular visitors to the sands of Miami Beach, these three stunning Miami women made the trek to the Palm Beaches sometime in 1918 or 1919 to bask in the glow of the famous (and infamous) who frequented Palm Beach, well before Miami became the epicenter of Florida's international fame. From left are Joyce Cohen, Myrna Meyers (it was said that Myrna Loy, the famed actress, was named for this Myrna because of her great beauty and serene countenance), and Joyce Schrager.

On the shores of Lake Worth, a golfer
practices her drive as she prepares to tee off
on the Palm Beach course.

Palm Beach County extends well to the west, encompassing the communities on the east side of Lake Okeechobee as well as South Bay at the "bottom" of the lake. One east-side community, Chosen, was reachable only by poor roads or by boat on the Hillsboro Canal when this photograph was made in 1922. A fishing and farming community, its railway station actually had "Belle Glade" on one side and "Chosen" on the other, the FEC referring to the two communities as one in its timetables.

FROM A ROAR TO A LIMP

(1920–1929)

One of the most vicious gangs of robbers and thugs in the United States was the infamous Ashley gang that robbed banks and businesses in Palm Beach County and farther north. The outlaws even held up an FEC train. Fortunately for the people of Florida, Sheriff Bob Baker, a steely eyed, no-nonsense lawman, would be instrumental in bringing the desperados to justice.

The western edge of the county is replete with agricultural communities including Belle Glade-Chosen, Canal Point, Pahokee, and South Bay. This photograph from the 1920s shows beans from the Lake Okeechobee growing region being unloaded at the eastern end of the West Palm Beach Canal.

On March 18, 1925, the second Breakers fire occurred, this one far more damaging than the one of June 1903. The winter season would end within a week, but the hotel was still open, ensuring a fairly large guest count. Following the conflagration, the hotel was rebuilt, and the third Breakers, a marvel of concrete and steel construction, is still thriving today.

As Clematis Street grew in importance, and traffic increased dramatically, parking in the center of the roadway was discontinued, and curbside parking instituted instead. Here, in 1924, with the great Florida boom in full sway and no thoughts that a "bust" was even remotely possible in the near future (it would come beginning in late 1926) a crowd is gathering at the Edward Roody Real Estate office. This view faces west on Clematis from Narcissus Avenue.

The third Breakers would open to grand acclaim, the all-concrete structure no longer a fire hazard. Here, the stunning beauty of the new hotel's lobby lounge is evident. It is still a glamorous destination for travelers from throughout the world today.

The Olive was one of West Palm Beach's early hotels catering primarily to business travelers. Most likely located on Olive Avenue, the hotel is shown in 1925 in a photograph taken by Pownall Studio.

Following Flagler's death, his widow, Mary Lily Kenan Flagler, would marry Judge Robert "Bob" Worth Bingham, later associated for many years with the Louisville *Courier-Journal* newspaper. In 1917, she died under mysterious circumstances. The estate put Whitehall up for sale, and it was eventually purchased by a group that turned it into a hotel of the same name. It did not return to the Flagler heirs until Henry Flagler's granddaughter, Jean Flagler Matthews, purchased the property, formed a foundation, and had the hotel torn down. The home, dedicated to the memory of Henry Flagler, is now a museum bearing his name.

Looking east across Lake Worth, this late 1920s view shows both the Royal Poinciana (directly in front of the camera) and the Whitehall Hotel at right. The Poinciana would be torn down in the early 1930s, a victim of age and its wooden construction.

Once the Whitehall Hotel opened, the owners, much to their credit, made every effort to maintain a first-class operation. One elegant example, shown here, was the sculpture in the patio of the hotel, maintained with fresh flowers on a daily basis.

By 1925, Clematis had become the principal business street of West Palm Beach and Palm Beach County, thriving in the heart of the Florida boom. Among its stores were Max Sirkin's men's furnishings; Sam Sable, clothier; and the hat store of Joseph Schupler. The Seaboard Railway ticket office is on the left.

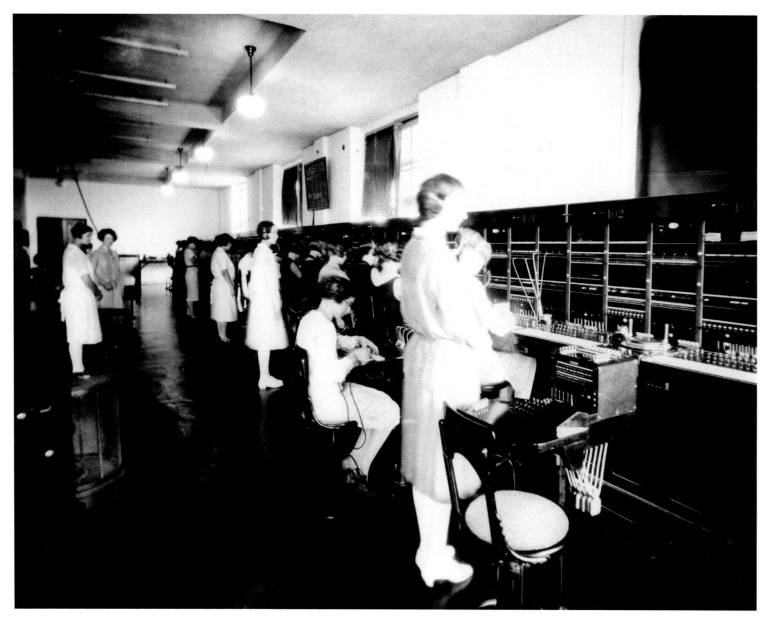

By 1926, long-distance telephoning was a way of life. In order to handle the ever-increasing volume of calls thrust upon it by the great boom of the 1920s, Southern Bell installed a brand-new long-distance switchboard in West Palm Beach, responsible for all Palm Beach County long-line calls. At least ten operators are visible in the photo.

Another victim of the 1926 hurricane was the sailboat *Marchioness,* stranded over a seawall at Palm Beach. The 1926 storm was one of four disasters that led Florida into the "bust" that was the harbinger of the worldwide Great Depression, which began three years later.

The 1926 storm (this was before hurricanes were named; they were simply known by the dates of landfall) wreaked immeasurable damage on Palm Beach County. Ralph W. Moore, of Wakulla, Florida, was serving as Seaboard Air Line depot ticket agent when the storm hit and is shown here walking around the parking area of the Florida Motor Coach Line garage. Many of the buses were damaged beyond repair.

Shown around 1927, the Northwood Office sign dominates this scene, with McCreary's Drugs at left. The Maddock Building, at right, was home to a number of offices and small stores.

On March 10, 1927, "A. E. Z.," "Chas.," and "Mgr. Rader" are standing in front of Charley's Cafe, adjacent to the Olive Hotel. It is possible that "Chas." is the Charley of Charley's Cafe and the two unidentified men second and third from left are the cooks.

Olive Avenue is the cross street shown at the next intersection. That corner, Clematis and Olive, was one of West Palm's busiest. Prominent in this view are the Western Union office and Sable's Shoe Store. For shopping and commerce, Clematis was to West Palm what Flagler Street was to Miami.

For many years, passenger trains were allowed on the island of Palm Beach, but automobiles were not. Later, of course, the prohibition ended, but well into the 1940s the pedicabs, almost always driven by an African-American, were a Palm Beach staple, and for many, the main mode of transport.

Taken in 1927 by Resler Photo Studio, this fine image is of the Kettler Theatre (left) and the Citizen's Bank (right). A Florida coconut palm frond graces the upper left of the photo.

A close-up of the employees of the Palm Beach Bottling Works does not identify any of them except James E. Cook, fifth from left. The man at right is apparently a manager but is not identified in the photo.

The Palm Beach Bottling Works was the home of Nu-Grape and Orange Crush, among other warmly recalled soft drinks. In this image taken by the H. S. Bell Photo Company, the man seventh from left is identified as James E. Cook.

This March 19, 1930, photo shows only a minimal number of people enjoying the shores of Palm Beach County, once packed with winter season visitors. The beaches would remain essentially empty until the Great Depression eased late in the decade.

Into the Depths of Depression

(1930–1939)

This woman was photographed March 19, 1930, next to the giant roots of a 38-year-old bombax ceiba, commonly called a silk cotton tree, red silk tree, and other names. This giant was planted in 1892 on the grounds of the Royal Poinciana Hotel.

The FEC bridge, just visible at the left edge of this 1930 picture, will be gone by 1935. The Royal Poinciana is in the center with the Whitehall Hotel to the south (right) of it. Across the island from the RP is The Breakers, which stands as stately today as it did then.

Even during the height of the Great Depression, many golfers found the means to continue playing. Pictured here, just prior to tee off, are noted Palm Beach duffers William F. Kenny, M. Tennes, Lewis Smith, and Edwin M. John.

Through the Federal Emergency Relief Administration and other agencies, tax dollars were funneled by the federal government to communities across America during the depression. The West Palm Beach area received funds to provide nursery services for children, including the boys and girls photographed here on May 6, 1935.

Another Palm Beach County FERA project was assistance in building Morrison Field, an airport which opened in December 1936. In World War II, it would become an Army Air Force base. Following the war, on August 11, 1948, Morrison Field became Palm Beach International Airport. Construction work was in its early stages when this photo was taken on May 3, 1935.

A crew was photographed April 30, 1935, constructing the Sherman Point drawbridge, one of the local opportunities created by FERA's efforts to provide out-of-work Americans with employment.

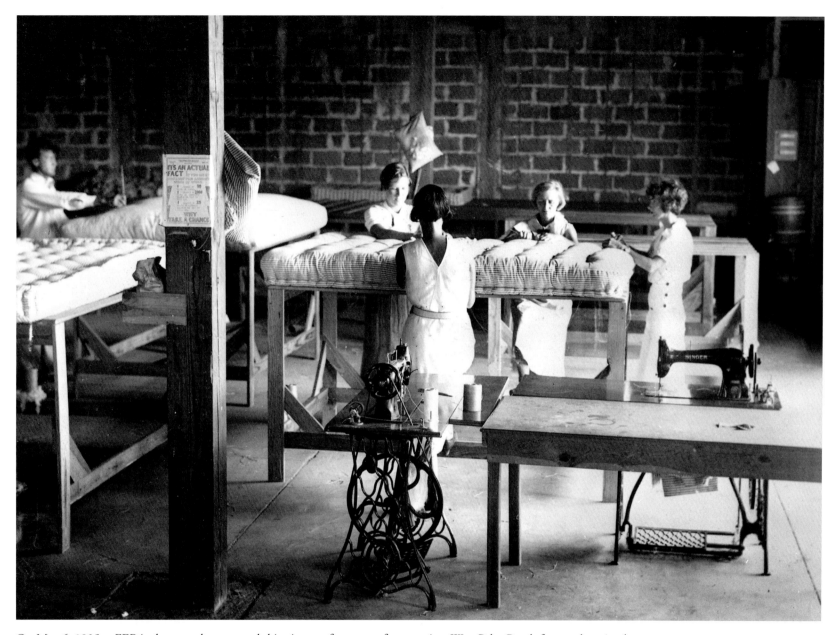

On May 6, 1935, a FERA photographer snapped this picture of a group of women in a West Palm Beach factory, learning how to prepare a mattress for shipping.

In a close-up view, several women are completing the mattress-building task and going through the final quality-control steps prior to boxing the finished product.

As part of its mission, FERA assisted cities and towns with community enrichment projects. The West Palm Beach parks and recreation department showed off its new City Park open-air auditorium, complete with band shell and facilities, shortly after completion. This photo was made May 2, 1935.

Through a photography project, FERA and other government agencies documented depression-era life. Taken in 1935, this photo was made at Green Acres Nursery School in West Palm Beach. The children, for the most part, appear oblivious to the fact that their see-saw ride was being recorded for posterity.

West Palm Beach High School maintains a proud tradition as a great educational facility in Palm Beach County, and generations of Palm Beachites are proud to have been "Wildcats." Even in 1935, the school was having growing pains. This April 30 FERA image recorded a new addition as it neared completion.

On May 1, 1935, local schoolchildren enjoyed the day with games and entertainment at West Palm Beach's Phipps Park.

Although commercial air service had not yet reached the Palm Beaches, far-sighted individuals recognized that the day would soon be at hand. On May 3, 1935, this surveying team was laying groundwork for the eventual building of what would, in 1948, become Palm Beach International Airport.

Colonel Edward R. Bradley owned and operated the beach club and casino at Palm Beach. The elegance and glamour of the club were a match for the swankiest of gaming emporiums anywhere in America or Europe, and it remained in business long after gaming was constitutionally outlawed in Florida. Bradley's was for many years a Palm Beach landmark.

The Seaboard Railway began diesel-electric, streamlined passenger train service from Penn Station, New York, to Miami a full year ahead of its great competitors, the Atlantic Coast Line–Florida East Coast Railway combination. The companies dueled endlessly for the New York–to–Florida passenger business. In December 1938, just prior to the beginning of service, the Seaboard exhibited its new locomotives and streamliner equipment. The platform with West Palm Beach's station name appears just to the right of the nose of the diesel.

A Sleeping Giant Awakened

(1940–1949)

Lake Worth looks calm in this 1941 Charles Foster photograph of the Palm Beach Biltmore, but storm clouds in Europe and Asia are about to envelop America.

On January 13, 1941, the SS *Manhattan,* a 24,000-ton luxury liner of the United States Lines, sailing perilously close to the Florida mainland, suddenly ran aground 300 yards off the coast, nine miles north of Palm Beach. After sitting helplessly for 22 days, she was finally freed by the Coast Guard Cutter *Mojave* on February 4, 1941. The *Manhattan,* rechristened *Wakefield,* became a troop transport vessel in World War II.

Photographs of Colonel Edward R. Bradley are rare. He was a horseman who owned Idle Hour Farm in Lexington, Kentucky, and, of course, he was the proprietor of Bradley's Beach Club. Shown here in 1943 with his Afromobile driver, he appears well relaxed as he takes a break from the rigors of hospitality management.

The Styx had changed dramatically from its previous incarnation by the time this photograph was made by Resler Photo Studio in 1941.

In 1946, Elsie Anderson and Florence Lainhart, two Palm Beach beauties, posed for a cheesecake-style photo. The image, captured by a Florida Department of Commerce photographer at West Palm Beach, was intended for use in State of Florida publicity campaigns.

Elegant, high-quality browsing and buying have long been the order of the day on Worth Avenue or any other shopping street in Palm Beach. The cars, palm trees, and beautiful buildings tell the story of one of America's most desirable destinations.

The Florida Department of Commerce was, for many years, responsible for Florida's tourism and business promotion and never missed an opportunity to glamorize every part of the state. The beauty of Palm Beach was perfect for these publicity gambits. The private yacht *Southward-Ho* was used often to show people enjoying the Intracoastal Waterway and Lake Worth.

Even the banks on Palm Beach bespoke elegance and refinement. In 1946, it was important to show stability and safety, with the memory of the Great Depression still fresh in the public mind.

Although not quite like today's "drive-through banking," the First National Bank of Palm Beach arranged to open a window so that patrons would not have to actually come into the bank, although they did have to exit their cars. As this 1946 photograph shows, customers could "ring bell for service" at the Auto Teller window.

West Palm, across Lake Worth from Palm Beach in 1946, looks very much like the famous view of Miami across Biscayne Bay from Watson Island, proving the Palm Beaches could convey the same stunning "big city" image.

The Beach Boys may have memorialized California girls in their songs, but Florida's beaches have never lacked for beauties either, whether natives or tourists. Here famed Palm Beach photographer Dean Cornwell photographs Mrs. Hjordis Termesden, a Swedish visitor, in 1947.

Bethesda-by-the-Sea Episcopal Church is one of Palm Beach's oldest and most beautiful houses of worship. The bell tower shown here is one of Palm Beach's most recognizable landmarks.

Edward T. Stotesbury was a famed Philadelphia industrialist who died at the age of 89 in 1938. His widow, Eva R. Stotesbury, moved to their Palm Beach home, "El Mirasol," and following her death in 1946, the entire contents of El Mirasol were sold between February 25 and March 3, 1947, one of the greatest "house sales" in the history of Palm Beach County. Admission to the auction was $2, a sum—at the time—guaranteed to keep the less desirable away.

Among the items placed for sale at the El Mirasol auction were the estate's vehicles. At least six of them (and possibly more) were sold during the seven-day event.

A portion of the crowd at the Stotesbury auction is visible here. All of the men are in ties and jackets and most of the women are wearing the chapeaus of the day.

Worth Avenue, on Palm Beach, was and is one of the most glamorous shopping streets in America. With most of the stores and restaurants now open year-round, it is a busy and active destination, frequented by tourists and residents alike. For many years, shoppers from as far south as Key West and as far north as Daytona would make the trip to Palm Beach a grand, one-day excursion.

Locating an image that includes the name of a Palm Beach pedicab, or Afromobile, driver is a rare, memorable, and highly rewarding find. Pedaling the beautiful Elizabeth Harvel during the 1947 winter season is longtime pedicab professional Homer Bacon Smith. His service was often requested by those who appreciated his gracious demeanor and personal attention, as well as his fine sense of humor.

Yale crew members took time off to pose with Florida governor Millard Caldwell's daughters, Sue (left) and Sally (right). Seated from left are John Lawrence, Dick Olmsted, Bill Meyer, John Kingsbury, and Greg Gates. The two men kneeling at left are Don Cadle and Bob Perew. Standing are crew members Pete Peacock, George Carver, Jimmy Beggs, Stew Griffing, and Sty Lawn. The photograph was made on the grounds of the Everglades Club during the 1948 rowing regatta. It is likely the crew was feted there sometime during their stay.

Lake Worth was a spectacular setting for winter crew competition. Many northern schools' athletes were delighted beyond words to spend part of the winter in the glorious climate and surroundings of the Palm Beaches. On January 2, 1948 (coincidentally, the 118th anniversary of Henry Flagler's birth), Ivy League rivals Yale University and the University of Pennsylvania are matching stroke for stroke in this scene from one of their numerous rowing regatta matches.

The war had ended, and America was returning to normal in 1947. Famed artists Arthur William Brown (left) (1881–1966) and Russell Patterson (1896–1977) were photographed sketching Florence Kallender at the Coral Beach Club.

A 1946 view of Worth Avenue brings back memories of longtime retailers. Close to the camera is the Ted Stone wine and liquor store, popular with Palm Beach socialites. Next to it is the famous restaurant Ta-boo. Both have been gone for many years.

Ripley's junk, the *Mon Lei,* was often seen in Lake Worth and is shown here at one of the private piers. Robert Ripley of "Believe it or Not" fame purchased the junk in 1946. Its name means "infinity."

Pictured aboard the *Mon Lei* are Robert Ripley, his secretary Lisa Wisse, and his dog, Schlimiel. The photo was taken in 1947 in the junk's alcove.

By the late 1940s, fashion designers were using Palm Beach as a backdrop for the introduction of their newest designs. In 1948, at the Palm Beach Biltmore, Lily Dache introduced her newest creations. From left, model Joan Johnson, C. L. Larsen, Jean Depres (Ms. Dache's husband), and model Euvera Benway enjoy the Florida sun as well as the gala event. Mr. Depres was, at the time, an executive with fragrance manufacturer Coty Company.

In January 1948, the National Association of Chain Drug Stores held their yearly convention in Palm Beach. Among the celebrities in attendance was the then-famous, 47-inch-tall "Johnny" (Johnny Roventini, 1912–1998) who was known for his highly starched bellhop uniform complete with pillbox hat and his stentorian "Call for Philll-lip Mohrrr-is!" cry. His national recognition reached such heights that he was hired to pull prize-winning tickets during the convention raffle, the gifts ranging from radios to boxes of fresh Florida fruit.

By 1946, when this photo was taken, West Palm Beach was the second-most important business center of South Florida and the Gold Coast, with only Miami having a larger and busier downtown. The city center would soon house a Burdine's department store as well as other well-known, high-volume retail outlets. This view is nothing if not pure nostalgia, for today not a single building shown still exists.

Thanks to this marvelous photograph, we *know* where Joe DiMaggio had gone to in January of 1948! On the 13th of that month, the famous "Yankee Clipper" was in West Palm Beach for "R 'n' R," and that morning he made his way to Bill McGowan's Umpire School to visit with friends. Shortly after arrival, he encountered three-year-old Larry Valencourt and took the time to show little Larry how to hold the bat.

On January 10, 1948, FEC 4-8-2-type steam locomotive Number 813 carried convention attendees to West Palm Beach aboard an excursion train, "The National Association of Chain Drug Stores Special." It is uncertain who took this photograph, but possibly it was longtime FEC Railway company photographer Harry M. Wolfe.

Still bundled in their winter finery, which they would soon shed, Mr. and Mrs. W. S. Marshall, of Cleveland, Ohio, detrain from the NACDS Special. The Marshalls, representing Cunningham Drug Company of Detroit, would later remark that they were unprepared for both the beauty of the surroundings and the hospitality that they encountered during the convention, and that they would return to Florida as soon as practicable.

The Breakers is the last of the Flagler System Hotels and remains an American icon. Photographed in 1949, this is the south tower of the front entrance of the hotel. Although minor changes have been made, the front remains very much the same today, the view recognizable immediately to anyone approaching the hotel from the west side.

Florence Lainhart of West Palm Beach became Florida's "Year Round Girl of 1947" and was seen nationally in the state's promotional advertising. The image of Florida as a winter-season-only resort was being discarded by hoteliers and business people who recognized that visitors could and would come to the sunshine state throughout the year.

Ray Bolger, best known for his portrayal of the Scarecrow in *The Wizard of Oz,* was an accomplished song-and-dance man. For the National Association of Chain Drug Stores' 1948 convention, Bolger was the headliner, shown here in the midst of a January 13 performance, following which he received a standing ovation.

In 1936, Claude D. Pepper (1900–1989) was elected to the U.S. Senate, where he would remain until defeated in 1950 by George Smathers. The 1950 campaign was particularly vicious. According to legend, Smathers accused Pepper of being an extrovert and having a sister who was a thespian, assuming rural voters wouldn't know the meaning of his words, but the story was probably a hoax. When Pepper's advertising Jeep was involved in a collision, Smathers' friend, Carl L. Hahn, sent Smathers this picture with a note that said, "Here's what is left of the Pepper machine in Palm Beach County!" Some years later, Pepper was elected to the U.S. Congress, representing a Dade County district.

CHANGE IN THE AIR

(1950–1959)

In 1951, the Florida State Chamber of Commerce held its 35th annual meeting in West Palm Beach. The keynote speaker was Florida governor Fuller Warren, shown here at the microphone. To his left is Florida's senior U.S. senator Spessard L. Holland.

The groundbreaking for Temple Israel in West Palm Beach in 1951 was "groundbreaking," indeed. The Palm Beach County Jewish community had always taken a back seat to that of Miami, so building a new temple was a great achievement for the Palm Beaches. Shown speaking is Norman Mirsky. From left are Rabbi Richard Singer, Harry Halpern, Philip Blicher, Alfred Fink, an unidentified man, Alice Gordon, O. P. Gruner, Louis Leibouit, another unidentified attendee, Leon Goldsmith, Mayor Jack Faircloth, and David Tisnower.

The majestic Jupiter Inlet Lighthouse remains active today. First lit on July 10, 1860, it is the oldest existing structure in Palm Beach County. During World War II, it was dimmed with a low-wattage bulb. Several ships were sunk offshore by Nazi submarines, and the sad duty of recovering bodies as they washed ashore fell to the lighthouse keepers. In 1959, the two-story lighthouse keeper's dwelling was torn down and new quarters were built. The lighthouse itself is a national historic landmark.

Glamour photography remained a mainstay of publicity and promotion for the state, particularly for its oceanfront and gulf coast areas.

Palm Beach County, in a major convention coup, hosted the Inter-American Tourism Conference, October 13-15, 1954, featuring events in both West Palm Beach and Palm Beach. Many attendees stayed at the Colony Hotel on Palm Beach. Here participants enjoy the closing banquet in the hotel's famed dining room.

Growth brings infrastructure improvements. This 1954 photograph shows that construction on Florida Power and Light's new generating plant at Riviera Beach was well under way.

Ever since the arrival of Henry Flagler's railroad and hotels, the Palm Beaches have been a magnet for the rich and famous, a stomping ground for politicians and celebrities. Participating in a celebrity golf tournament in the late 1950s, Florida's U.S. senator George Smathers, at far-left, is joined by the Duke of Windsor, who is holding a hat. The man to the right of the duke is believed to be the great "Slammin' Sammy" Snead, who loved Palm Beach and played here almost every winter throughout the 1950s. The man at far-right is unidentified and may be a tournament official.

The First Church of Christ, Scientist, at 138 Lakeview Avenue in West Palm, is a stately edifice which has been an area landmark for many years. Though the flora is different, the beautiful building remains as striking as ever.

Lee Petty (1914–2000), a NASCAR pioneer and the father of Richard Petty, drove in his first stock-car race at the age of 35 and in 1959 won the inaugural Daytona 500. In 1953, 39 years old, he is photographed in West Palm Beach with his Dodge, no. 42.

The Plantation Dining Room of The Famous Restaurant was a longtime gathering spot for Lake Worth's residents. Located at 912 Second Avenue North, the restaurant was known for both its food and excellent service.

In the mid-1950s, construction began on Florida's first turnpike, the 110-mile Miami–Fort Pierce Sunshine State Parkway, which opened in 1957. West Palm Beach was a major interchange and toll collection facility. In addition, a service plaza was built there. This 1956 image shows paving of the southbound roadway is in progress north of the WPB interchange. The northbound lanes had already been paved.

Stately and elegant, the Colony Hotel opened in 1947. Built in the modified Colonial style, it currently has 92 recently renovated and updated guest rooms and is a favored dining and dancing spot in the Palm Beaches. Shown here in 1955, the hotel has maintained a reputation for staff excellence and fine service.

Unlike much of Florida, where the view of the ocean or the gulf has been blocked by high rises and private beaches, Palm Beach maintains a policy of keeping the east side of its oceanfront drive open, just as it was in this 1956 Charles Barron photograph.

In the mid-1950s, when the Mass home was built on Everglades Island in Palm Beach County, it was not just modernistic, it was futuristic! A stunning piece of architecture in the style of Frank Lloyd Wright's work, the Mass house is shown here in 1956 in a photograph by Charles Barron.

When the Pratt & Whitney aircraft engine plant opened in 1958, eighteen miles northwest of West Palm Beach on State Road 710—the Bee Line Highway—it was an economic shot in the arm for the county, providing hundreds of jobs with millions of dollars in annual payrolls. This photo of the employees relaxing at lunch hour in the open-air courtyard was made in 1959.

Completed in 1957, the original Florida Turnpike (the Sunshine State Parkway) extended from Fort Pierce to Miami, with service and facilities plazas at Pompano, West Palm Beach, and Fort Pierce. The newly opened West Palm Beach Service Plaza is shown here in 1958. Francis P. Johnson, who did much of the Turnpike Authority's photo work, made this image.

The Brazilian Court opened for business on New Year's Day 1926 and became an instant "in-spot" for Palm Beachites and visitors alike. Located just off of Worth Avenue, the hotel currently has 80 rooms and a reputation for fine food and attentive service. In 1960, Palm Beach photographer Francis Johnson recorded one of the hotel's chefs presenting the tomato preparations of several famous chefs, with the beautiful background of the hotel dining room complementing the scene.

An Aura of Greatness Emerging

(1960–1967)

Built in 1901 by Henry Flagler for his third wife, Mary Lily (Kenan) Flagler, Whitehall was the couple's primary residence until his death in 1913. Later sold by the Flagler heirs, the home was turned into a luxury hotel with a tower built behind it. In 1959, upon learning that plans were in the works to raze the home, Flagler's granddaughter, Jean Flagler Mathews, formed a foundation and acquired the property, subsequently tearing down the hotel tower. In 1960, Whitehall was opened to the public as the Henry M. Flagler Museum.

Florida's only governor with a Harvard University law degree, Farris Bryant was elected in 1960. In this West Palm Beach photo, Bryant is at left, shaking hands with a constituent. Accompanying him, left to right, are Richard W. Ervin, Edwin L. Mason, Thomas D. Bailey, Ray E. Green, and J. Edwin Larson.

In 1962, Charles Barron photographed a group that went a-fishin' in the Atlantic off the coast of Palm Beach County in hopes of luring the elusive kingfish to their hooks.

In June 1962, photographer Charles Barron focused his lens on the new West Palm Beach Public Library, a facility much needed and long overdue at the time. Now one of Florida's largest and most modern libraries, in the 1960s, the fight to modernize and bring the library system up-to-date was a difficult struggle.

Three anglers proudly display their catch, a small sailfish, for the camera. This is another of the Charles Barron photos, taken in November 1961.

Whitehall's restored ceiling mural, decorations, and painting were strikingly captured by Charles Barron in February 1962.

As with most cities of note, West Palm Beach boasts an active and enthusiastic Chamber of Commerce, known today as the Chamber of Commerce of the Palm Beaches. This Barron photograph shows the Chamber building at 401 Flagler Drive in all its 1965 glory.

This 1965 exterior view of the Pratt & Whitney plant gives an idea of the size of this leading Palm Beach County employer. At the time it was constructed, the building shown was P & W's Florida Research and Development Center.

NOTES ON THE PHOTOGRAPHS

These notes, listed by page number, attempt to include all aspects known of the photographs. Each of the photographs is identified by the page number, a title or description, photographer and collection, archive, and call or box number when applicable. Although every attempt was made to collect all data, in some cases complete data may have been unavailable due to the age and condition of some of the photographs and records.